D1710525

INSIDE THE NBA

OKLAHOMA CITY
THUNDER

BY BRIAN MAHONEY

SportsZone

An Imprint of Abdo Publishing
abdobooks.com

abdobooks.com

Published by Abdo Publishing, a division of ABDO, PO Box 398166, Minneapolis, Minnesota 55439. Copyright © 2023 by Abdo Consulting Group, Inc. International copyrights reserved in all countries. No part of this book may be reproduced in any form without written permission from the publisher. SportsZone™ is a trademark and logo of Abdo Publishing.

Printed in the United States of America, North Mankato, Minnesota.
052022
092022

THIS BOOK CONTAINS RECYCLED MATERIALS

Cover Photo: Alex Goodlett/Getty Images Sport/Getty Images
Interior Photos: Melinda Nagy/Shutterstock Images, 1; Ronald Martinez/Getty Images Sport/Getty Images, 4, 38; Alex Brandon/AP Images, 6; Brett Deering/Getty Images Sport/Getty Images, 8, 11; Focus on Sport/Getty Images Sport/Getty Images, 12, 16, 22, 24, 34; AP Images, 15, 32; Ted S. Warren/AP Images, 18; Sue Ogrocki/AP Images, 21, 40; Dan Levine/AFP/Getty Images, 27; John Froschauer/AP Images, 28; Jacob Kupferman/ Getty Images Sport/Getty Images, 31; Mike Powell/Getty Images Sport/Getty Images, 37

Editor: Charlie Beattie
Series Designer: Joshua Olson

Library of Congress Control Number: 2021951681

Publisher's Cataloging-in-Publication Data

Names: Mahoney, Brian, author.
Title: Oklahoma City Thunder / by Brian Mahoney
Description: Minneapolis, Minnesota : Abdo Publishing, 2023 | Series: Inside the NBA | Includes online resources and index.
Identifiers: ISBN 9781532198380 (lib. bdg.) | ISBN 9781098272036 (ebook)
Subjects: LCSH: Oklahoma City Thunder (Basketball team)--Juvenile literature. | Basketball--Juvenile literature. | Professional sports--Juvenile literature. | Sports franchises--Juvenile literature.
Classification: DDC 796.32364--dc23

TABLE OF
CONTENTS

CHAPTER ONE
THE THUNDER
STORM BACK 4

CHAPTER TWO
FROM SONICS TO THUNDER .. 12

CHAPTER THREE
THUNDERBOLTS 22

CHAPTER FOUR
DAYS OF THUNDER 32

TIMELINE 42
TEAM FACTS 44
TEAM TRIVIA 45
GLOSSARY 46
MORE INFORMATION 47
ONLINE RESOURCES 47
INDEX 48
ABOUT THE AUTHOR 48

THE THUNDER STORM BACK

When fans showed up at Chesapeake Energy Arena for Game 6 of the 2012 Western Conference finals, they had already been through a storm. Fittingly, it was raining heavily in Oklahoma City, Oklahoma. Thunder and lightning boomed and flashed around the area. But that was nothing compared to the noise inside once the game started.

In its short time in the NBA, Oklahoma City had developed a reputation as a loud place to play. That was certainly true in Game 6, and for good reason. The fans, all clad in white T-shirts, were hoping the Thunder could seal a spot in the National Basketball Association (NBA) Finals.

Just a week earlier, that seemed unlikely. The San Antonio Spurs had thumped Oklahoma City in the first two games of the series. Led by superstars Tim Duncan and Tony Parker, the

Thunder forward Kevin Durant lays in two of his 34 points during Game 6 of the 2012 Western Conference finals.

Durant (35), James Harden (13), and Russell Westbrook formed one of the NBA's most talented trios during their time together in Oklahoma City.

Spurs were a tough opponent. They had won four NBA titles since the 1998–99 season.

Not only were the Spurs good, but they were also red hot. They had lost just five games since the beginning of March. After winning the first two against the Thunder, San Antonio held a 20-game winning streak. It had begun in early April, during the regular season. Now the calendar was turning to June.

Oklahoma City was no slouch, though. Forward Kevin Durant led the NBA in scoring in 2011–12. Guard Russell Westbrook was a triple-double threat every night. NBA Sixth

Man of the Year James Harden could score points in bunches off the bench. Now they had to find a way to win four of the next five. If the Thunder couldn't do it, their championship dreams were dashed.

TURNING THE TABLES

The road to Game 6 hadn't been easy. After their first two losses, the Thunder's trio of stars turned it on in Game 3. They combined for 47 points in a 102–82 Thunder victory. Durant then scored 36 points as Oklahoma City took Game 4. Game 5 was in San Antonio, where the Spurs were dominant. But Oklahoma City's three stars all had 20-point nights in another victory. Suddenly the tables were turned. Oklahoma City was one win away from the NBA Finals.

"We never thought these guys had an advantage over us, even though we had lost a few," Kevin Durant said of the Spurs after the Game 3 win.

The Thunder had called Oklahoma City home for only four seasons since moving from Seattle. But this was their second trip to the Western Conference finals. A year earlier the Thunder had bowed out to the Dallas Mavericks in five games.

As fans strolled through the rain into the arena for Game 6, they hoped for a different outcome. But the Spurs came out strong. They silenced the white-clad Oklahoma City crowd by rolling up an 18-point first-half lead. Durant's twisting,

Durant, *center*, scored 14 points in the third quarter of Game 6 as the Thunder erased a double-digit halftime deficit.

off-balance three-pointer at the halftime horn made it 63–48 San Antonio.

TAKING OVER

The shot was a sign of things to come. In the locker room, Thunder coach Scott Brooks urged his players to come out with more spirit in the second half. They did just that. Soon the Spurs' lead was dwindling. Westbrook and Durant were hitting shots from everywhere. The duo combined for 22 points in the third quarter alone.

As the Thunder inched back into the game, the noise in the arena rose higher and higher. Chants of "O-K-C!" echoed around the packed stands.

With 1:41 left in the quarter, Durant shook off his defender and drained a deep step-back three-pointer. The shot gave Oklahoma City a 79–77 lead. The crowd noise boomed throughout the arena.

The game stayed tight through the fourth quarter. With less than 30 seconds left, the Thunder led 105–99. The Spurs' Manu Ginobili heaved a three-pointer that bounced off the hoop. Harden squeezed it tight to his chest as the crowd roared again.

Duncan fouled Harden to extend the game. But the celebration had already started. Durant took a second to hug his mother and brother, who were seated in the first row. He knew the game was over.

The final was 107–99. The franchise had been to the NBA Finals three times while in Seattle. Now it was going back for the first time as the Oklahoma City Thunder. Even better, the team had erased a 2–0 series deficit against a seemingly unbeatable team. Then the Thunder had charged back from 18 down to win Game 6. Even the defeated Spurs were impressed.

"We had a great run," Ginobili said. "We just couldn't beat these guys."

Durant salutes the crowd in the final seconds of Oklahoma City's victory over the San Antonio Spurs in Game 6.

CHAPTER TWO

FROM SONICS TO THUNDER

The story of the Thunder began far away from their Oklahoma City home. In 1960–61 the NBA had only eight teams. Most of them played in the eastern United States. But basketball was becoming more popular. The league quickly started adding new franchises all over the country.

One of the earliest expansion years was 1967. That year two teams entered the league—the San Diego Rockets and the Seattle SuperSonics. The Rockets moved to Houston shortly after. But basketball took off in the Pacific Northwest.

The team took its name from the aviation industry. Seattle is home to the Boeing Corporation, which manufactures airplanes. In the late 1960s the company had a contract to create a jet that could travel at incredible speed. It was known as a "supersonic" jet. Team owner Sam Schulman liked the name and adopted it for the city's new team. The jet never

Seattle SuperSonics guard Slick Watts drives for a layup against the Washington Bullets.

took off, as the project was canceled. But the SuperSonics stuck around on the court.

Early fans of the team did not see too many wins. Despite solid players like Bob Rule, Lenny Wilkens, and Spencer Haywood, the team struggled early on. The Sonics went 23–59 in their first season, when they allowed more than 125 points per game. That is still one of the worst defenses in NBA history.

CHAMPIONS

It took Seattle eight NBA seasons to make the playoffs. The Sonics finally broke through after the 1974–75 season. But the team took off three years later. It started the 1977–78 season slowly. At one point its record was 5–17. Seattle brought in former player Lenny Wilkens as head coach, and he engineered a quick turnaround. The Sonics went 42–18 the rest of the season. They ended the year in the NBA Finals but lost in seven games to the Washington Bullets.

Wilkens returned as coach the next year, and the Sonics were among the NBA's best teams. Led by a young trio that included guards Dennis Johnson and Gus Williams and center Jack Sikma, they went back to the Finals. Seattle faced the Bullets again. This time the tables were turned. The Sonics blew away Washington in five games and claimed their first NBA title.

Coach Lenny Wilkens, *left*, and guard Fred Brown hold up the Larry O'Brien Trophy after Seattle's NBA championship in 1979.

With a great coach and young players, Seattle looked like an emerging dynasty. But the 1980s belonged to the Los Angeles Lakers. The Sonics watched as their rivals from California played in eight NBA Finals. Seattle shrank back out of playoff contention.

Shawn Kemp attempts a reverse during the Dunk Contest at the 1990 All-Star Game.

RETURN TO GREATNESS

The team's fortunes did not change until the early 1990s. By then Seattle had two new stars in guard Gary Payton and forward Shawn Kemp. In 1993–94 Seattle won its first division title in 15 years. Led by coach George Karl, the Sonics topped the Pacific Division again in three of the next four seasons.

The playoffs were a different story. The Sonics made it out of the second round only once in that stretch. In 1995–96 Payton and Kemp led them all the way to the NBA Finals. There they fell in six games to legendary guard Michael Jordan and the Chicago Bulls.

By the early 2000s Seattle was a struggling franchise in more ways than one. The team wasn't winning. But the bigger problem was their home arena. KeyArena had been home to the team since it was founded. Even though it had been renovated in the mid-1990s, the venue was considered small and old fashioned.

Team owner Howard Schultz hoped the city could help pay for upgrades. By 2006 it was clear that was not going to happen. Schultz opted to sell the team. The new owners were led by Clay Bennett, a businessman from Oklahoma City. Bennett also tried to ask the city of Seattle for help renovating KeyArena but was turned down. He then asked the NBA for permission to move the team.

Clay Bennett, *right*, bought the SuperSonics in 2006 and moved them to Oklahoma City two years later.

A NEW HOME

Despite being one of the city's most beloved teams, the SuperSonics left Seattle after the 2007–08 season. Bennett brought them to his hometown in Oklahoma. But Seattle asked the NBA to leave the name "SuperSonics" in case a new NBA team ever came to town. That meant Oklahoma City needed a new name.

The area around Oklahoma City is known as "Tornado Alley." Violent thunderstorms are common there. The name "Thunder" was officially announced as the nickname in September 2008.

The squad that moved to Oklahoma City was struggling on the court. During the final Seattle season, the Sonics finished 20–62. The first season in Oklahoma was not much better. The Thunder started the 2008–09 season with a 3–29 record. They improved but still finished 23–59.

However, the team had some young stars. Forward Kevin Durant was drafted before the team's final season as the SuperSonics. Guard Russell Westbrook was drafted just before the team relocated. With another high draft pick in 2009, the Thunder added guard James Harden.

The trio turned the Thunder around immediately. Oklahoma City improved to 50–32 in 2009–10. The next year the Thunder played in the Western Conference finals. A trip to the NBA Finals was next, in 2012.

That trip to the Finals ended in defeat. The powerful Miami Heat knocked off Oklahoma City in five games. it was the highlight of an incredible start to the team's newest chapter. In all, the Thunder made the playoffs in 10 of 11 seasons from 2009–10 to 2019–20. They did it even though star players kept leaving.

Sonics Go, Storm Stay

Clay Bennett also bought the Seattle Storm of the Women's National Basketball Association when he purchased the SuperSonics. However, he ended up selling them back two years later, in 2008, to a group that kept them in Seattle. The Storm won their fourth WNBA title in 2020.

Harden was traded to the Houston Rockets in 2012. Four years later Durant left as a free agent. Westbrook kept the team competitive before he was also traded to Houston in 2019.

By the 2020–21 season, the Thunder had run out of top talent. They had their first losing season since 2008–09, their first year in Oklahoma City. Team president Sam Presti made several trades to stockpile draft picks over the coming seasons. The hope was that the team could unearth a new generation of young stars and get back to the top.

An NBA Preview

The Thunder were not the first team to play in Oklahoma City. Because of damage done by Hurricane Katrina in 2005, the New Orleans Hornets were unable to play in their home city. They temporarily relocated to Oklahoma City for the 2005–06 and 2006–07 seasons. They were officially known as the New Orleans/Oklahoma City Hornets for those two years.

Guard Russell Westbrook won the NBA MVP Award after the 2016–17 season.

CHAPTER THREE

THUNDERBOLTS

In both Seattle and Oklahoma City, the team has featured some of the NBA's biggest stars. The first was point guard Lenny Wilkens. He was already a five-time NBA All-Star when he joined the Sonics before the 1968–69 season. Wilkens reached the game in three of his four seasons in Seattle.

By his second year with the team, he was the head coach as well as a star player. Wilkens left Seattle in 1972 to finish his playing career. After retiring as a player, Wilkens returned to Seattle and coached the Sonics for parts of eight more seasons. He led the Sonics to the NBA Finals twice and won the title in 1979.

As Seattle became more competitive in the mid-1970s, guard Fred Brown developed into the team's key scoring threat. His outside shot was so deadly he earned the nickname "Downtown" Freddie Brown in high school. The nickname

Guard Fred Brown spent his entire 13-year career with the Seattle SuperSonics before retiring in 1984.

Seattle's backcourt combination of Gus Williams (1) and Dennis Johnson (24) was one of the NBA's best in the late 1970s.

stuck. By the time Seattle was in the NBA Finals, he was coming off the bench. But Brown was still the Sonics' captain. He played his entire career with Seattle and scored 14,018 points. That was the team record until 2000.

THE SUPER SUPERSONICS

Two younger guards started over Brown on Seattle's championship team. Gus Williams led the team in scoring during every game of their victory in the 1979 Finals. "The Wizard," as he was known, scored 36 points in Game 4, a 114–112 overtime win for the SuperSonics.

Point guard Dennis Johnson was coming off the bench when Wilkens took over as head coach in 1977. One of his first ideas was to put the young guard in the starting lineup. Seattle took off when Wilkens made the switch. Johnson was a tough defender. He was also a clever player. Later in his career he won two more titles while playing for the Boston Celtics. His teammate in Boston, the great forward Larry Bird, called Johnson "the smartest player I ever played with."

Rounding out the roster was Hall of Fame center Jack Sikma. Most centers at the time were lumbering players who would back their defenders down. Sikma did almost the opposite. He would catch the ball and immediately spin to face his defender. The maneuver eventually became known as "the Sikma Move." He could then drive or pull up for his deadly accurate jump shot. Sikma used it to score more than 12,000 points in nine seasons with Seattle.

GEORGE, GARY, AND SHAWN

By the time the Sonics were title contenders again, they had two new stars and another great coach. George Karl took over a team that was 20–20 halfway through the 1991–92 season. He led them to a 27–15 record the rest of the way to reach the playoffs. Karl made the playoffs each of the next six seasons as well. He left Seattle after the 1997–98 season, having won 72 percent of his games.

A big reason for those wins was point guard Gary Payton. He was a solid scorer, but he was also a dynamic defender. His ability to stick to opposing guards earned him the nickname "the Glove." Payton led the NBA in steals while leading Seattle to the NBA Finals in 1995–96. Payton was also one of the best trash talkers in the NBA. He loved to try to rattle his opponents.

"If I started locking up somebody, then I'd start talking even more and I'd talk more aggressive," Payton explained.

Teaming with Payton was powerful forward Shawn Kemp. He came to the NBA straight from a Texas community college in 1989. After taking a year to get adjusted, Kemp became a must-see player. At 6 feet, 10 inches tall and 230 pounds, Kemp was an incredible athlete with powerful dunking skills.

Kemp's most famous slam came during the 1992 NBA playoffs. After collecting a pass at the top of the key, Kemp drove the lane. Golden State Warriors center Alton Lister tried

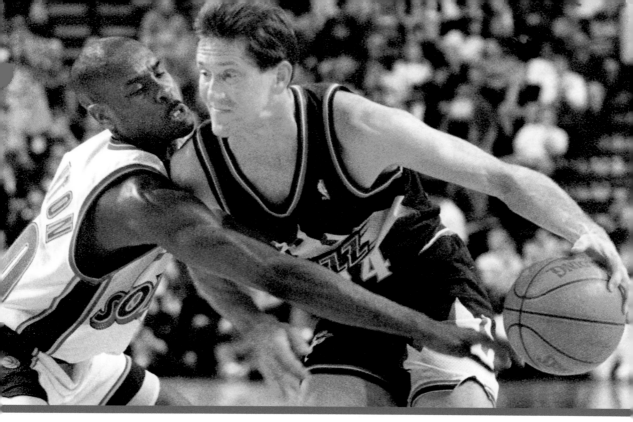

Hall of Fame guard Gary Payton, *left,* was known for his relentless, physical defense.

to get in his way. Kemp nearly jumped over Lister, sending the defender flying as he threw down a one-handed dunk. As he came down, Kemp crouched and pointed both index fingers in Lister's direction.

THREE YEARS TO A BIG THREE

Kevin Durant helped change the game with his gifts during the 2000s. Durant also stood 6 feet, 10 inches tall. But instead of Kemp's powerful build, Durant had long, skinny arms. He was also incredibly skilled for a big man.

Kevin Durant, *left,* **celebrates with teammate Donyell Marshall during the SuperSonics' final game in Seattle.**

Players Durant's size often spend most of their time closer to the hoop. Durant wasn't most players. A graceful shooter, he could hit three-point shots as well as most guards. Yet he could also beat any big man to the basket. That combination made him one of the most unstoppable scorers in NBA history. The "Slim Reaper" won his first league scoring title in just his third season.

Durant was drafted in June 2007, while the team still played in Seattle. He helped usher in the Oklahoma City era, but he had some notable help. With the team still struggling, it drafted guard Russell Westbrook in 2008. He soon emerged as a historically good all-around player. In NBA history, only guard Oscar Robertson of the Cincinnati Royals (a team that later became the Sacramento Kings) had averaged a triple-double for a whole season. In 2016–17 Westbrook became the second.

Even with Westbrook and Durant together, the Thunder did not get close to the playoffs in 2008–09. Once again they had a high draft pick. And once again general manager Sam Presti struck draft gold. James Harden started only seven games during his three years in Oklahoma City. But the guard was one of the best bench players in the league. By the time Oklahoma City reached the NBA Finals in 2012, Harden was the league's Sixth Man of the Year.

Steven Adams

One of Oklahoma City's key role players in the 2010s was center Steven Adams. When the Thunder picked him in the 2013 draft, Adams made history. He was the first player from New Zealand ever taken in the first round of the NBA Draft.

Having three superstar players on the roster created a problem. The Thunder could not afford them all. Harden proved to be the odd man out. The Thunder traded him to the Houston Rockets in 2012. The team was never as successful with just two stars. And Durant left after the 2015–16 season to sign with the Golden State Warriors. Fans in Oklahoma City were angered by the move. The Warriors already had one of the best teams in the NBA. Thunder fans accused Durant of quitting on them to join a team that didn't really need him.

With just Westbrook left, the guard shone. But even after adding star forward Paul George as a free agent, the team could not compete with the Western Conference's best teams. Westbrook was eventually shipped to Houston for another great point guard, Chris Paul. The Thunder also used the move to start piling up draft picks. They received four of them for trading Westbrook. The 2019 trade that sent George away netted the Thunder five more.

The team added young guard Shai Gilgeous-Alexander to the roster in the George trade. Gilgeous-Alexander quickly blossomed into a reliable scorer. He was also the leader of a youth movement that Oklahoma City hoped would carry it back to the postseason.

Oklahoma City guard Shai Gilgeous-Alexander averaged 23.7 points per game during the 2020–21 season.

CHAPTER FOUR

DAYS OF THUNDER

These days, the sight of teenage players in the NBA is common. That was not always the case. Former Seattle SuperSonics forward Spencer Haywood was a huge reason the NBA became a young man's game.

Haywood joined Seattle in December 1970. He averaged a double-double in four of his five seasons with the team. However, his biggest impact on the NBA came not on the court but in the courtroom.

At the time league rules said a player had to be four years out of high school before they could play in the NBA. The rule was designed to steer players into college basketball. Haywood spent one year at the University of Detroit. But he wanted a pro career after that. The NBA did not allow him to join. Instead he signed up with the Denver Rockets of the rival American Basketball Association.

Seattle forward Spencer Haywood dunks during a game against the Cleveland Cavaliers in 1972.

Guard Dennis Johnson, *left,* scored in double figures during every game of Seattle's 1979 playoff run.

After one season in Denver, Sonics owner Sam Schulman tried to sign Haywood up anyway. Schulman simply ignored the NBA's rule and gave Haywood a contract. The two men took the NBA to court. In March 1971 the United States Supreme Court took their side. As a result, the NBA changed its rule. Soon, more players started entering the NBA at an earlier age. By the year 2000 it was common for players to jump straight to the NBA from high school. In 2005 the league adjusted its rule once again. Now players must be at least 19 years old to be eligible for the NBA Draft.

D. J.'S REDEMPTION

Dennis Johnson was one of the biggest reasons the Seattle SuperSonics were in the 1978 NBA Finals. His stifling defense paired well with backcourt mate Gus Williams's scoring. The pair paced Seattle to a 42–18 record down the stretch after a slow start. In the Finals, Johnson starred at both ends of the court through the first five games. He averaged more than 20 points per game. In Game 3 of the series, the 6-foot-4-inch point guard blocked seven shots. Seattle took a 3–2 lead into Game 6. Needing just one more win, the city was ready to celebrate its first professional sports title since 1917.

The Sonics needed Johnson to continue his production to close things out. He could not. Johnson shot 4-for-16 from the field and finished with only nine points in Game 6. The Bullets blew out Seattle 117–82.

Game 7 back in Seattle was even worse. Johnson took 14 shots in the game. He missed all of them. He finished with four points and watched the Bullets celebrate a title.

Johnson admitted he played terribly. He also told reporters he would make the most of another chance. He only had to wait a year. Seattle was back in the 1979 NBA Finals. The Washington Bullets were waiting for them again.

Johnson made good on his promise. He averaged 22.6 points per game. In the fifth and final game, Johnson's 21

Historic Three-Pointer

Dennis Johnson left Seattle after the 1979–80 season. But not before he made NBA history. The three-point shot was new to the NBA that season. In the opening game of the Western Conference semifinals, Seattle trailed the Milwaukee Bucks 113–111 with six seconds remaining. Johnson took an inbounds pass and sprinted to the three-point line. Leaning forward as he jumped, Johnson hit the shot. It was the first game-winning three-pointer in playoff history. It was such a new concept, many people watching the game thought he had only tied the score.

points were second only to Williams's 23. The victory on Washington's home floor clinched Seattle's title. Johnson was named the Most Valuable Player (MVP) of the Finals.

AN UNEXPECTED YEAR

Seattle fans did not have many reasons to cheer during the 1980s. But more than 34,000 fans had a big one at the 1987 All-Star Game. The annual matchup was held at Seattle's football and baseball stadium, the Kingdome. One of the game's starters was SuperSonics forward Tom Chambers. On a roster that included Hall of Famers Magic Johnson, Kareem Abdul-Jabbar, and Hakeem Olajuwon, Chambers stole the show. His 34 points led all scorers, and Chambers was named MVP.

Chambers and his teammates weren't done giving Seattle fans unexpected thrills in 1987. The team finished 39–43 and barely made the playoffs. As the seventh seed they were not

Forward Dale Ellis, *left,* **averaged 28.9 points per game during Seattle's upsets of Dallas and Houston during the 1987 playoffs.**

expected to last. But led by Chambers, guard Dale Ellis, and forward Xavier McDaniel, Seattle upset the Dallas Mavericks in round one.

Kevin Durant, *right,* posts up against Miami's LeBron James during Game 5 of the 2012 NBA Finals.

They followed that up with another Texas-sized upset. They knocked out the Houston Rockets in six games. Seattle was the lowest seed ever to reach the Western Conference finals. The run ended there at the hands of the mighty Los Angeles Lakers. But it was a special few weeks in the Pacific Northwest.

FROM SEATTLE TO OKLAHOMA CITY

That good feeling was gone by the end of the 2007–08 season. Fans knew their beloved team was leaving for Oklahoma City. They still turned up to fill KeyArena for a game against Dallas.

Fans serenaded their team with the same chant all game. "Save our Sonics!" echoed down from the stands. Rookie forward Kevin Durant waved his arms from the court to encourage the fans. He admitted later the scene nearly brought tears to his eyes. But Durant held it together. His back-to-back field goals in the final minute gave Seattle the lead for good in a 99–95 victory.

Durant didn't leave his clutch play in Seattle. After his shooting display against the San Antonio Spurs in the 2012 Western Conference finals, the Thunder welcomed the Miami Heat to Oklahoma City. The Heat controlled the game throughout the first half and led by 13 at one point. Durant seemed to be missing. He took only one shot in the second quarter.

Russell Westbrook picked up the slack for his teammate in the third. He led all scorers with 12 points in the quarter. With 16 seconds left he drove to the hoop for a layup. Even though he was fouled on the shot, he still scored. Then he knocked down the free throw for a 74–73 lead. It was the Thunder's first lead of the game.

Russell Westbrook, *right*, is congratulated by Oscar Robertson after Westbrook broke Robertson's record for triple-doubles in a season.

Durant did the rest. He found his offensive rhythm in the fourth quarter and buried 17 points. In his new home, fans chanted "MVP!" at Durant. The Thunder pulled away for a 105–94 victory and a series lead.

TRIPLE THREAT

After Durant left the Thunder in 2016, it was Westbrook's turn to take center stage. In his first season without his dynamic teammate, Westbrook stepped up his game. The guard had always been a good scorer. He steadily became a better passer and rebounder. In 2016–17 he put all three skills together.

He showed off his talents early in the season. On October 28, 2016, the Thunder were taking on the Phoenix Suns. The game went to overtime. When it was over, Westbrook had 51 points, 13 rebounds, and 10 assists in a 113–110 victory. It was the first 50-point triple-double in the NBA since 1975. It was also a sign of things to come.

The NBA Shuts Down

The Thunder were warming up for a home game against the Utah Jazz on March 11, 2020, when the players were suddenly pulled off the floor. Jazz center Rudy Gobert had tested positive for COVID-19. The game was canceled, and the NBA suspended its season that night.

Westbrook scored 50 points and recorded a triple-double two more times that season. The last came on April 9, 2017, against the Denver Nuggets. It was Westbrook's forty-second of the season. That broke the record for triple-doubles in a season set by Oscar Robertson in 1961–62.

Westbrook also led the NBA in scoring. His final stat line was 31.6 points per game, 10.7 rebounds, and 10.4 assists. No player had averaged a triple-double since Oscar Robertson in 1961–62. For his efforts, Westbrook was named the NBA's MVP.

He continued to carry the team through the 2018–19 season. Twice more Westbrook averaged a season-long triple-double. But his trade in July 2019 meant the last of Oklahoma City's three stars were gone. It was time for a new generation to take over.

TIMELINE

1967

The Seattle SuperSonics begin their first season. They finish the year with a 23–59 record.

1975

The SuperSonics make the playoffs for the first time after finishing 43–39. Seattle beats the Detroit Pistons in the first round before losing to the Golden State Warriors in six games.

1978

Seattle reaches the NBA Finals for the first time. The Sonics lose 4–3 to the Washington Bullets.

1979

The SuperSonics win their only NBA championship. They beat the Bullets 4–1 to avenge the loss from the season before.

1987

Seattle reaches the Western Conference finals despite a 39–43 record. The Sonics are the first number seven seed to make it that far.

1994

Seattle finishes 63–19 but becomes the first number one seed to lose to a number eight seed in the playoffs after falling 3–2 in an opening-round series against the Denver Nuggets.

1996

Defensive Player of the Year Gary Payton leads Seattle to the NBA Finals. The SuperSonics lose 4–2 to Michael Jordan and the Chicago Bulls.

2006

The SuperSonics are sold to a group led by Oklahoma City businessman Clay Bennett.

2007

Seattle drafts Kevin Durant with the number two pick in the NBA draft.

2008

The NBA Board of Governors approves relocation of the SuperSonics to Oklahoma City.

2012

The Thunder lose to the Miami Heat in the NBA Finals, then trade James Harden before the start of the next season.

2016

Oklahoma City loses a 3–1 lead against Golden State in the Western Conference finals. Kevin Durant joins the Warriors after the season.

2017

Russell Westbrook is voted NBA MVP after averaging a triple-double for the season.

2021

The Thunder finish 22–50. It is Oklahoma City's first losing record since 2008–09, its first season after moving from Seattle.

FACTS

FRANCHISE HISTORY
Seattle SuperSonics
(1967–2008)
Oklahoma City Thunder
(2008–)

NBA CHAMPIONSHIPS
1979

KEY PLAYERS
Ray Allen (2003–07)
Fred Brown (1971–84)
Tom Chambers (1983–88)
Kevin Durant (2007–16)
Dale Ellis (1986–91, 1997–99)
Shai Gilgeous-Alexander
(2019–)
James Harden (2009–12)
Spencer Haywood (1971–75)
Dennis Johnson (1976–80)
Shawn Kemp (1989–97)
Rashard Lewis (1998–2007)
Chris Paul (2019–20)
Gary Payton (1990–2003)
Jack Sikma (1977–86)
Russell Westbrook (2008–19)

Lenny Wilkens (1968–72)
Gus Williams
(1977–80, 1981–84)

KEY COACHES
Scott Brooks (2008–15)
George Karl (1991–98)
Lenny Wilkens
(1969–72, 1977–85)

HOME ARENAS
KeyArena (1967–78, 1985–94,
1995–2008)
Known as:
Seattle Center Coliseum
(1967–78, 1985–94)
Kingdome (1978–85)
Tacoma Dome (1994–95)
Paycom Center (2008–)
Formerly known as:
Ford Center (2008–10)
Oklahoma City Arena
(2010–11)
Chesapeake Energy Arena
(2011–2021)

TEAM
TRIVIA

AN ALL-TIME GREAT

The NBA announced a list of the top 50 players and top 10 coaches in history in 1997 for its 50th anniversary. Lenny Wilkens was the only player voted to both.

GOING HOME AGAIN

Chris Paul played twice in Oklahoma City, for two different teams. He was on the Hornets when they played there from 2005 to 2007 because of damage in New Orleans from Hurricane Katrina. He played for the Thunder in 2019–20.

WHEELING AND DEALING

The Thunder made 11 trades during the 2020 offseason. That was an NBA record.

AGELESS WONDER

Paul had 19 points, 12 assists, and 11 rebounds in Game 7 of the 2020 Western Conference opening round against the Houston Rockets. At 35 years, 119 days old, he was the oldest player to record a triple-double in a Game 7.

GLOSSARY

assist
A pass that leads directly to a basket.

aviation
Associated with the making and flying of airplanes.

contender
A person or team that has a good chance at winning a championship.

double-double
Accumulating 10 or more of two certain statistics in a game.

dynamic
Energetic and exciting; in sports, usually referring to an athlete with one or more outstanding skills.

dynasty
A team that has an extended period of success, usually winning multiple championships in the process.

expansion
The addition of new teams to increase the size of a league.

franchise
A sports organization, including the top-level team and all minor league affiliates.

layup
A shot made from close to the basket; an easy shot.

rebound
To catch the ball after a shot has been missed.

seed
A rank assigned to a team in a tournament.

triple-double
Accumulating 10 or more of three certain statistics in a game.

MORE INFORMATION

BOOKS

Abdo, Kenny. *History of Basketball.* Minneapolis, MN: Abdo Publishing, 2020.

Mahoney, Brian. *GOATs of Basketball.* Minneapolis, MN: Abdo Publishing, 2022.

Ybarra, Andres. *Great Basketball Debates.* Minneapolis, MN: Abdo Publishing, 2019.

ONLINE RESOURCES

Booklinks
NONFICTION NETWORK
FREE! ONLINE NONFICTION RESOURCES

To learn more about the Oklahoma City Thunder, please visit **abdobooklinks.com** or scan this QR code. These links are routinely monitored and updated to provide the most current information available.

INDEX

Abdul-Jabbar, Kareem, 36
Adams, Steven, 29

Bennett, Clay, 17–18, 19
Bird, Larry, 25
Brooks, Scott, 9, 10
Brown, Fred, 23–25

Chambers, Tom, 36–37

Duncan, Tim, 5, 9
Durant, Kevin, 6–7, 9–10, 19–20, 27–30, 39–40

Ellis, Dale, 37

George, Paul, 30
Gilgeous-Alexander, Shai, 30
Ginobili, Manu, 9–10
Gobert, Rudy, 41

Harden, James, 7, 9, 19–20, 29–30
Haywood, Spencer, 14, 33–34

Johnson, Dennis, 14, 25, 35–36
Johnson, Magic, 36
Jordan, Michael, 17

Karl, George, 17, 26
Kemp, Shawn, 17, 26–27

Lister, Alton, 26–27

McDaniel, Xavier, 37

Olajuwon, Hakeem, 36

Parker, Tony, 5
Paul, Chris, 30
Payton, Gary, 17, 26
Presti, Sam, 20, 29

Robertson, Oscar, 29, 41
Rule, Bob, 14

Schulman, Sam, 13, 34
Schultz, Howard, 17
Sikma, Jack, 14, 25

Westbrook, Russell, 6, 9, 19–20, 29–30, 39–41
Wilkens, Lenny, 14, 23, 25
Williams, Gus, 14, 25, 35–36

ABOUT THE AUTHOR

Brian Mahoney has been a national NBA writer for the Associated Press since 2005, covering the NBA Finals, All-Star Games, and international basketball events such as the Olympics and basketball world championships. Based in New York, Mahoney covers the Knicks and Nets, along with providing coverage of boxing and tennis events. He is a 1995 graduate of the University of Connecticut, where he started his career covering the women's basketball team that won the national championship.